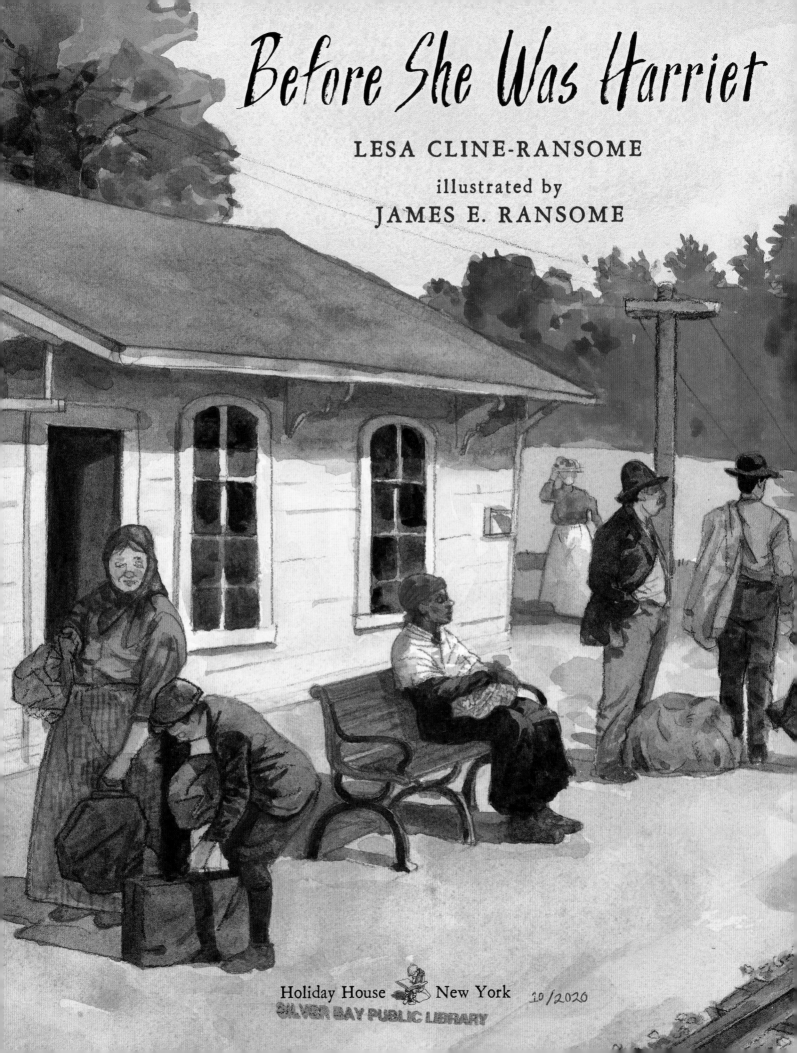

Before She Was Harriet

LESA CLINE-RANSOME

illustrated by
JAMES E. RANSOME

Holiday House ❦ New York 10/2020

Here she sits
an old woman
tired and worn
her legs stiff
her back achy

but before wrinkles formed
and her eyes failed
before she reached
her twilight years
she could walk for miles
and see clearly
under a sky lit only with stars

Before she was an old woman
she was a *suffragist*
a voice for women
who had none
in marriages
in courts
in voting booths
before her voice became
soft and raspy
it was loud
and angry
rising above injustice

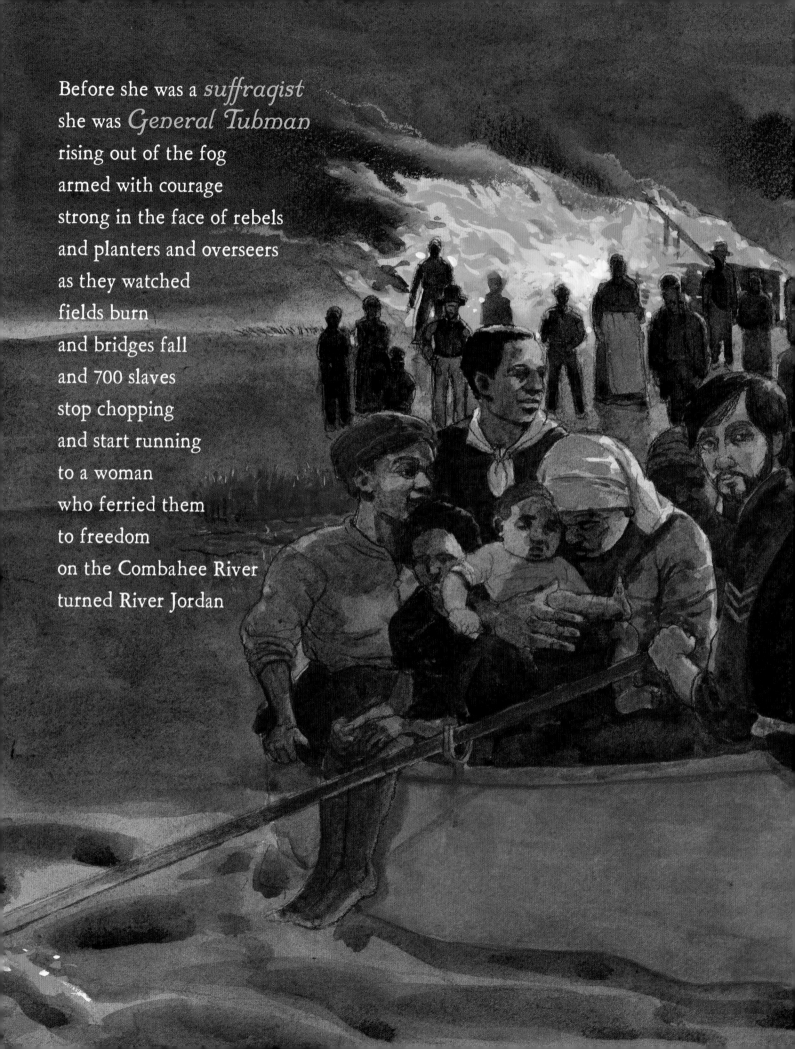

Before she was a *suffragist*
she was *General Tubman*
rising out of the fog
armed with courage
strong in the face of rebels
and planters and overseers
as they watched
fields burn
and bridges fall
and 700 slaves
stop chopping
and start running
to a woman
who ferried them
to freedom
on the Combahee River
turned River Jordan

Before she was
General Tubman
she was a *Union spy*
carrying secrets
across battlefields
to soldiers
fighting in the Civil War
for President Lincoln
to end slavery

Before she was a
Union spy
she was a *nurse*
caring for those hit
with bullets
and hatred
and fear
tending to them
with bandages
and words
in the bloodied dirt of
southern soil

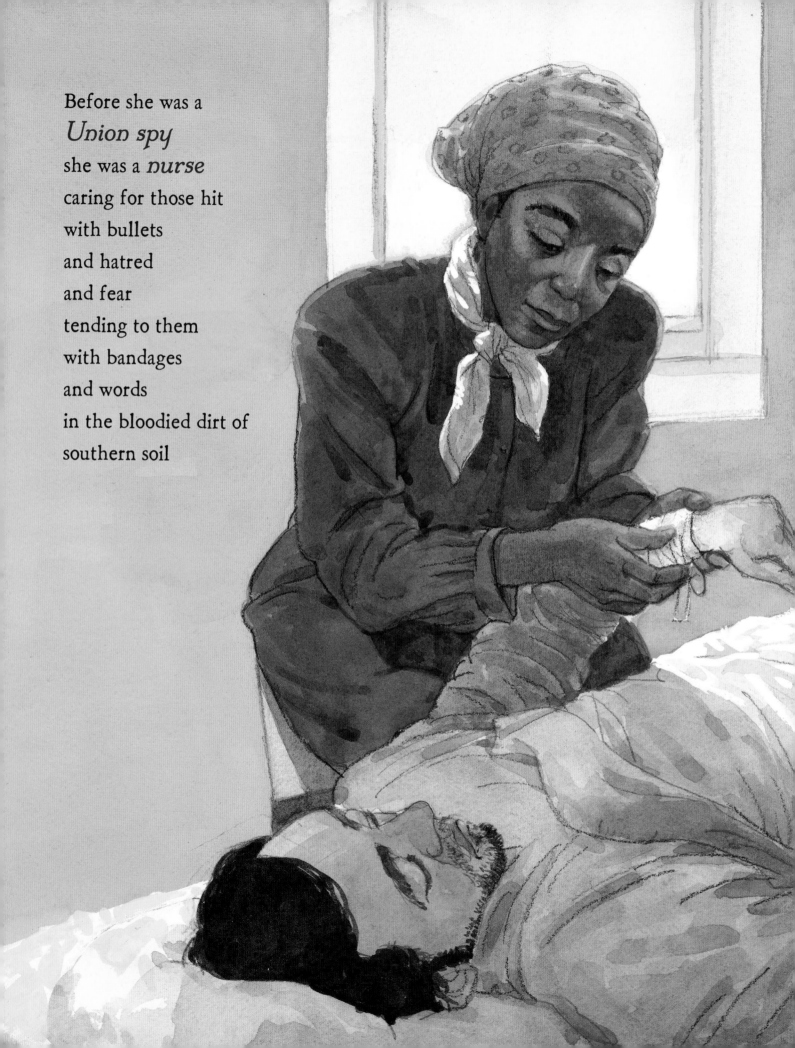

Before she was a *nurse*
she was *Aunt Harriet*
daughter of Ben and Rit
who helped her parents
flee their master
and find their way
through woods and streams
to the safety of Canada
and a new home
in the north

Before she was *Aunt Harriet*
she was *Moses*
a conductor
on an Underground Railroad
with no trains
and no tracks
just passengers
traveling to freedom
up north
through swamps
past slave catchers
across rivers
under the cover of night

seeking the promised land
for her people
led by dreams
and God
and faith
a wisp of a woman
with the courage
of a lion

Before she was *Moses*
she was *Minty*
of Maryland
of one slave owner
and then others
who worked her
punished her
with lashes
broke her back
but not her spirit

Before she was *Minty*
she was *Araminta*
a young girl
taught by her father
to read
the woods
and
the stars
at night
readying
for the day

she'd leave behind
slavery
along with her name
and pick a new one
Harriet

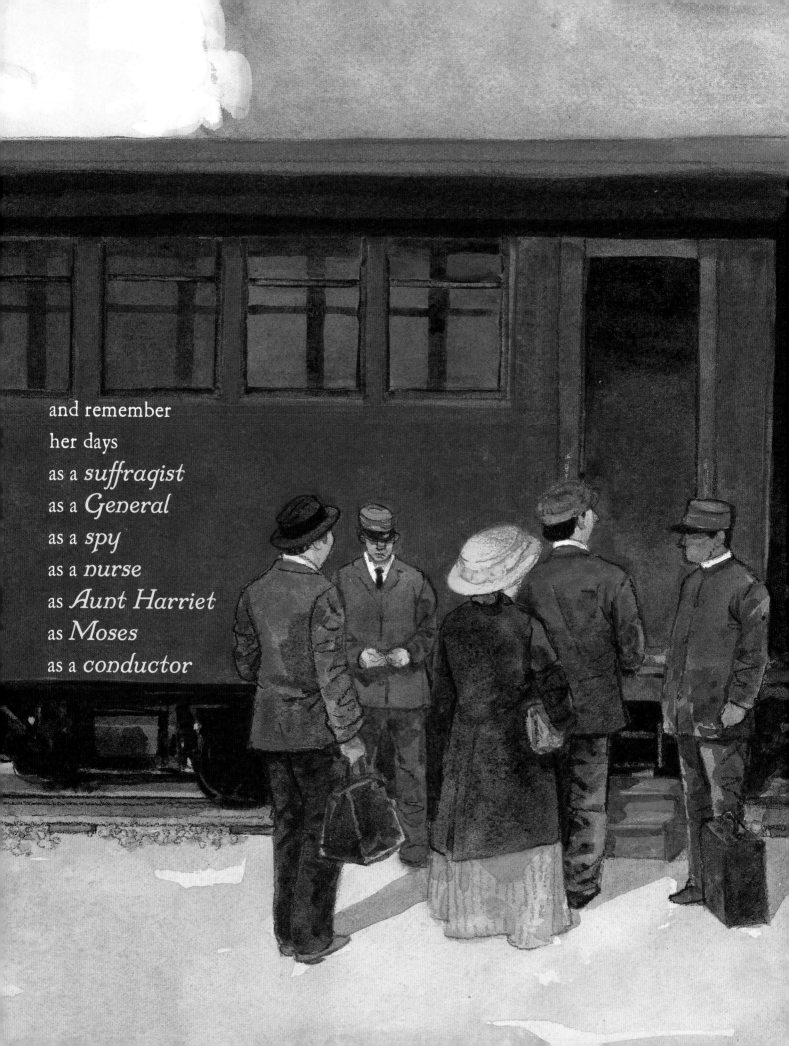

and remember
her days
as a *suffragist*
as a *General*
as a *spy*
as a *nurse*
as *Aunt Harriet*
as *Moses*
as a *conductor*

as *Minty*
as *Araminta*
who dreamed
of living long enough
to one day
be old
stiff and achy
tired and worn and wrinkled
and *free*

A Note about Sources

Much of the information I gathered for this book was found in Beverly Lowry's *Harriet Tubman: Imagining a Life*. Her book led me to other invaluable resources including Catherine Clinton's *Harriet Tubman: The Road to Freedom* and Kate Clifford Larson's *Bound for the Promised Land: Harriet Tubman, Portrait of an American Hero*.

Two hundred miles from my home, in Auburn, New York, I visited the Harriet Tubman National Historical Park. For nearly forty years of her life, Harriet lived in the home she purchased in 1857 from her friend and neighbor William Seward, the United States Senator from New York. Years later she purchased an adjoining parcel, where, with the help of the African Methodist Episcopal Zion Church, she established the Tubman Home for Aged & Indigent Negroes. In 2017, the home and church were designated National Historical Parks. Harriet is buried nearby in the Fort Hill Cemetery.

Two of the finest picture books on the life of Harriet Tubman are Carole Boston Weatherford and Kadir Nelson's *Moses: When Harriet Tubman Led Her People to Freedom* and Alan Schroeder and Jerry Pinkney's *Minty*. These titles were used as mentor texts and, after the publication of *Before She Was Harriet*, for comparative purposes in my presentations, to illustrate the various ways one story can be told from multiple points of view.

Additional online resources

Harriet Tubman Museum & Educational Center:
visitdorchester.org/harriet-tubman-museum-educational-center/

Harriet Tubman Home for Aged & Indigent Negroes: www.nps.gov/places/tubmanagedhome.htm

National Underground Railroad Freedom Center: freedomcenter.org/enabling-freedom/history

History for Kids: www.historyforkids.net/underground-railroad.html

Educator's Guide: holidayhouse.com/docs/Before_She_Was_Harriet_Revised_0917.pdf

10/2020

To the guiding force of all the women who have led the way through courage, strength, perseverance, and intellect—Harriet Tubman, Sojourner Truth, Fannie Lou Hamer, Toni Morrison, Michelle Obama, Viola Davis, Anne Sneed, Ernestine Cline—L. C.-R.

To black women who have carried the weight of family and work with grace and dignity—J. R.

Text copyright © 2017 by Lesa Cline-Ransome • Illustrations copyright © 2017 by James E. Ransome • All Rights Reserved
HOLIDAY HOUSE is registered in the U.S. Patent and Trademark Office • Printed and bound in June 2019 at Toppan Leefung, DongGuan City, China. • www.holidayhouse.com • First Edition • 7 9 10 8

Library of Congress Cataloging-in-Publication Data • Names: Cline-Ransome, Lesa, author. | Ransome, James, illustrator.
Title: Before she was Harriet : the story of Harriet Tubman / by Lesa Cline-Ransome ; illustrated by James Ransome.
Description: First edition. | New York : Holiday House, [2017] | Audience: 004–008. • Identifiers: LCCN 2016051680 |
ISBN 978-0-8234-2047-6 (hardcover) • Subjects: LCSH: Tubman, Harriet, 1820?–1913—Juvenile literature. | Slaves—United States—Biography—Juvenile literature. | African Americans—Biography—Juvenile literature. | African American women—Biography—Juvenile literature. | Underground Railroad—Juvenile literature. • ISBN 978-0-8234-4429-8 (paperback)